A·LITTLE
New Orleans
Cookbook

Norma MacMillan

ILLUSTRATED BY
CATHY HENDERSON

Chronicle Books

First published in 1995 by
The Appletree Press Ltd, 19–21 Alfred Street,
Belfast BT2 8DL
Tel. +44 (0) 1232 243074
Fax +44 (0) 1232 246756
Copyright © 1995 The Appletree Press, Ltd.

First published in the United States in 1995
by Chronicle Books, 275 Fifth Street,
San Francisco, California 94103

ISBN 0-8118-0906-4

9 8 7 6 5 4 3 2 1

Introduction

A local saying goes "There are two times of day in Louisiana — mealtime and in-between." It's certainly true in New Orleans where dining well has always been a way of life. Even in the early days, when it was just a walled city of mud streets and open gutters surrounded by a cypress swamp, its more prosperous residents enjoyed fine food and wines imported from France.

The cosmopolitan cuisine was originally based on Gallic, Hispanic, Afro-Caribbean, and Native American traditions, but it has absorbed many other influences, from the Cajun style of cooking that evolved separately in the bayou country to the succeeding waves of peoples from other European countries, the Americas, and Asia.

The climate in New Orleans is semi-tropical, and the hot sultry summers with sudden heavy rainstorms ensure that the locally grown fruits and vegetables are tasty and succulent. Combined with abundant fresh seafood and game, smoked spicy hams and sausages, exotic flavorings and volatile spicing, it's no wonder that New Orleanians eat so well and are so proud of their city's cuisine.

A note on measures
Spoon measurements are level. Seasonings are often to taste, but be adventurous. Recipes are for four unless otherwise indicated.

The New Orleans Breakfast

It's not difficult today to imagine the teeming bustle at the Mississippi riverbank of late nineteenth century New Orleans. A stream of boats would be docked, loading and unloading their cargoes. The merchants and tradesmen would have started their day before dawn, with just a cup of strong chicory coffee and a *beignet*. Little wonder that they had appetites which demanded a breakfast in the grand style.

Jackson Square is where goods were originally bought and sold, and the nearby French Market provided the coffeehouses, cafés, and restaurants. Many of the coffeehouses were open from early until late – the Creoles came here after church and after the opera. The merchants could have enjoyed their *petit déjeuner* of *café au lait* and *beignets* at the Café du Monde, which has been open 24 hours a day every day since the 1860s.

The Cotton Exposition of 1884–5 confirmed New Orleans as a center of commerce for the emerging South, and the big breakfast seemed to match the expansive and optimistic spirit of the day. Breakfast dishes such as *grillades* and grits, fancy omelettes and richly sauced poached eggs became an essential part of traditional Creole cuisine. The first popular breakfast place was Madame Bégué's, established over a century ago. Today, the place to go for breakfast is Brennan's, where it is claimed that 750,000 poached eggs are served each year.

Eggs Sardou

Created at Antoine's in 1908, in honor of the French dramatist Victorien Sardou who was a dinner guest, this very rich poached egg dish has become a New Orleans breakfast classic.

---

4 large cooked artichoke hearts
2 tbsp butter
10oz frozen chopped spinach, thawed and drained
2 tsp flour
$^2/_3$ cup whipping cream
2 tsp Herbsaint or Pernod
salt, black pepper, and grated nutmeg to taste
4 freshly poached eggs
$1^1/_4$ cups warm hollandaise sauce

Put the artichoke hearts in a small buttered baking dish and warm in the oven at 300°F. Meanwhile, melt the butter in a frying pan and sauté the spinach, stirring, until hot and excess liquid has evaporated. Sprinkle over the flour and stir in, then add the cream, liqueur, and seasoning. Cook, stirring, until thickened. Spoon the creamed spinach on to the center of 4 warmed plates. Nest an artichoke heart in each mound of spinach and top with a poached egg. Spoon the hollandaise sauce over the egg and serve immediately.

Beignets

Beignets with *café au lait* (made with strong chicory coffee) are a New Orleans institution. These sugar-dusted doughnuts are enjoyed all day in the French Market coffeehouses.

---

2 tsp dried yeast
1/2 cup warm water
1/2 cup sugar
1/2 tsp salt
1 egg, beaten
3/4 cup evaporated milk
2 tbsp butter or lard, melted and cooled
about 3 cups all-purpose flour
oil for deep frying
confectioners' sugar
(makes approx. 36)

In a medium bowl, dissolve the yeast in the water. Add the sugar, salt, egg, evaporated milk, and butter. Mix in enough of the three cups of flour to make a soft, but not sticky, dough. Knead until smooth and elastic. Leave to rise in a warm place until doubled in bulk. Punch the dough down, then knead again briefly. Roll out to a rectangle about 1/4 inch thick. Cut into 3 x 2 inch diamonds. Lay them on a lightly oiled baking sheet, cover and leave to rise until doubled in height. Deep fry in oil heated to 365°F until puffed and golden brown all over. Drain on paper towels. Serve fresh, sprinkled generously with confectioners' sugar.

Calas

"*Belle cala! Tout chaud!*" was the cry that could once be heard in the early mornings in the French Quarter. It was the *cala* lady, in a gingham dress and starched white apron, with her basket of hot, sweet, rice fritters, to be enjoyed with the first cup of *café au lait*. Note that the rice must be cooked one day in advance.

½ cup long-grain rice
2½ tsp dried yeast
½ cup warm water
3 eggs, beaten
½ tsp salt
½ tsp vanilla extract
6 tbsp sugar
1½ cups all-purpose flour, approx.
¼ tsp freshly grated nutmeg
oil for deep frying
confectioners' sugar for sprinkling
(makes approx. 36)

Cook the rice in unsalted water for 25–30 minutes until very soft and mushy. Drain and cool until warm. Dissolve the yeast in the warm water. Add to the rice and beat well to mash the rice. Cover and leave in a warm place overnight. Beat in the remaining ingredients. Add more flour, if needed, to make a thick batter. Cover and leave in a warm place for 30 minutes. Deep fry large spoonfuls of the batter in oil heated to 375°F until puffed and golden brown all over. Drain on paper towels. Serve fresh, sprinkled with confectioners' sugar.

Creole Cuisine

Defining Creole cuisine is almost as difficult as defining the Creoles themselves. Creole society in New Orleans originally comprised just the white descendants of the French and Spanish colonists. But the French-speaking free people of color, many of whom came to New Orleans from Santo Domingo (now Haiti) in the aftermath of the slave rebellions, also called themselves Creoles. Today, the term Creole embraces all people descended from French, Spanish, and Africans, both settlers and slaves.

Throughout much of the nineteenth century, New Orleans was a cosmopolitan French city, and all the wealthy Creole families had black cooks. These women, when called upon to prepare European style food, gave it their own special magic. In the culinary traditions of their native Africa, spices bought from Arab traders were widely used and ingredients such as okra were much loved. The resulting style of cooking was enjoyed in private homes, grand hotel dining rooms, and boardinghouses (which is how the famous Antoine's began) all over the French Quarter.

The Civil War ended the Creole way of life, but the cuisine became fashionable all over the city as the newly arrived Yankee entrepreneurs succumbed to its exotic flavors. Creole cuisine today is very sophisticated and elegant, yet is also enhanced with a flourish of Spain and spicing of Africa.

Turtle Soup

Spicy and rich, turtle soup is a New Orleans institution. Unlike turtle soups made in other parts of the South, this recipe is based on a well-cooked *roux* and is flavored with smoked ham, tomatoes, garlic, and sherry. Fresh turtle meat is very perishable and is not easy to get, but canned meat is fine for this soup.

---

6 tbsp butter	¼ tsp dried thyme
4 tbsp flour	1 bay leaf
1 onion, chopped	salt and black pepper to taste
1 small celery stalk, chopped	1 lb turtle meat (fresh, frozen, or
1–2 garlic cloves, finely chopped	canned), cut into ¾ inch cubes
2 tbsp chopped fresh, flat-leaf	2 tsp Worcestershire sauce
parsley	2 tsp lemon juice
4 oz smoked ham, diced	4 tbsp dry sherry
1 can chopped tomatoes	3 hard-boiled eggs, pushed through
approx. 5 cups rich beef stock or	a sieve, and grated lemon zest,
canned beef consommé	to garnish
¼ tsp ground allspice	

(serves 6–8)

Melt the butter in a large heavy pot, add the flour and cook, stirring, over low heat until this *roux* is the color of peanut butter. Add the onion, celery, garlic, parsley, and ham, and sauté until the vegetables are soft and translucent, stirring frequently. Add the tomatoes, stock, spices, herbs, and seasoning. Mix well, then add the turtle meat. Bring to a boil. Leave to simmer gently, half covered, for 1–1½ hours or until the turtle meat is tender, stirring occasionally.

Stir in the Worcestershire sauce, lemon juice, and sherry. Simmer for a further 5 minutes. Check the seasoning. Garnish each serving with sieved egg and a pinch of grated lemon zest. If the soup is too thick for your taste, add a little more stock before stirring in the Worcestershire sauce.

Shrimp Rémoulade

This seafood appetizer has a highly-seasoned vinaigrette-style *rémoulade*, unlike the French mayonnaise-based *rémoulade*. You'll find shrimp *rémoulade* on almost every restaurant menu in New Orleans. The sauce at Galatoire's is considered to be the finest.

1/2 cup chopped spring onions or scallions
1/2 cup chopped celery
2–3 parsley sprigs
1 large garlic clove
2 tsp hot paprika
2 tsp prepared horseradish
4 tbsp Creole or German mustard
1/2 cup white wine vinegar
3/4 cup olive or vegetable oil
Tabasco
sugar
salt, and black pepper to taste
1 1/2 lb freshly boiled and peeled shrimp or prawns
shredded lettuce to serve
(serves 6)

Lightly blend the spring onions, celery, parsley, and garlic in a food processor or blender. Whisk together the paprika, horseradish, mustard, and vinegar in a bowl. Gradually whisk in the oil. Add the

green purée. Season to taste. Pour the sauce into a bowl. Add the shrimp and stir. Cover and chill for at least 3 hours. Serve on shredded crisp lettuce.

Panéed Veal

People in New Orleans love to cook, eat, and talk about food. There are many versions of the same dish, each cook adding his or her own touches. This simple dish is an exception, and it is one of the most popular and traditional veal dishes on New Orleans restaurant menus.

---

1 ½ lb veal rump or round, cut into ³/₈ inch slices
flour
salt and freshly ground pepper
2 eggs, beaten with 2 tbsp cold water
fine, dry breadcrumbs
butter and oil for frying
lemon wedges to serve

Cut the slices of veal into rectangles about 3 x 4 inch. Pound with mallet until very thin and almost doubled in size. Season the flour. Coat each piece of veal lightly with seasoned flour and shake off excess, then dip in the egg mixture. Finally, coat with breadcrumbs, pressing to help them adhere. As the pieces of veal are coated, lay them out in one layer. Leave to dry for at least 10–15 minutes. Heat a mixture of butter and oil in a large skillet and fry the slices of veal in batches until golden brown and crisp on both sides. Drain on paper towels and serve hot, with lemon wedges.

Trout Amandine

The two all-purpose fish in New Orleans are redfish (a member of the bass family) and speckled trout. Despite its name, the speckled trout is really a weakfish, related to the drums and croakers. In this recipe it's topped with a browned butter sauce and toasted almonds – a New Orleans favorite.

---

4 skinned speckled trout fillets (or use grouper,
perch, or whiting), or 8 fillets from smaller fish
milk
flour
salt, black pepper, and cayenne pepper to taste
vegetable oil for pan frying
1/2 cup unsalted butter
3/4 cup flaked almonds
2 tbsp lemon juice
Tabasco sauce to taste

Cover the fillets with milk and soak for 20 minutes. Mix flour with the seasonings. Drain the fillets and coat with seasoned flour. Heat 1/4 inch of oil in a skillet over moderate heat until very hot. Fry the fillets for 2–4 minutes on each side or until golden brown and just cooked. Remove and keep warm. Pour all the oil from the skillet and wipe it clean, then melt the butter. Add the almonds. Cook until the butter begins to turn brown and smells nutty and the nuts are golden brown. Stir in the lemon juice and Tabasco. Spoon the sauce over the fish and serve.

Daube

The Creoles felt no qualms about using French names for their own culinary inventions! Take this beef pot roast, larded with spiced salt pork. For Daube Glacé, put a pig's foot in the pot (or add gelatine to the stock) and set the shredded beef, vegetables, and stock in a deep mold; slice thickly and serve with French bread.

$1/2$ tsp each ground cloves, allspice, and dried thyme
salt, black pepper, and cayenne pepper to taste
2 tbsp finely chopped garlic
4 oz salt pork fat, cut into small short sticks
4–5 lb piece of beef for pot roasting
3 tbsp lard or vegetable oil
2 onions, halved and sliced
3–4 carrots, thinly sliced
1 cup red wine
5 cups beef stock or water
chopped parsley and bay leaf
(serves 8–12)

In a bowl, using fingertips, mix the spices, thyme, seasonings, and half the garlic together. Toss the pork fat sticks in this mixture. Make deep incisions in the beef and insert the seasoned pork fat sticks. Heat the lard in a large heavy pot and brown the beef on all sides. When beef is browned remove from pot and set aside. Add the sliced vegetables and remaining garlic to the pot and brown well. Pour in the wine and bring to a boil, stirring. Return the beef to the pot and add enough stock to cover. Add some parsley and a bay leaf. Cover and simmer very gently for $2^{1}/_{2}$–3 hours or until the beef is tender. Cut into thin slices for serving.

Creole Stewed Tomatoes with Okra

The Spanish took the tomato to the Old World from the New then reintroduced it to the New World in Louisiana. In the rich alluvial soil, tomatoes grow big and juicy, and Creole cooks have long enjoyed the flavor that tomatoes give to all kinds of dishes.

---

1 lb ripe tomatoes (use canned tomatoes
when fresh ones are not at a seasonal peak)
2 tbsp butter
2 onions, halved and sliced
1–2 garlic cloves, finely chopped
$1/2$ tsp each sugar
$1/2$ tsp dried basil
Tabasco
salt, and black pepper to taste
1 lb baby okra, left whole

If the tomatoes have tough skins, peel them. Chop the flesh, scraping out the seeds and juice into a bowl. Strain all the juice from the seeds and reserve it (discard the seeds). In a saucepan, melt the butter and fry the onions until soft. Add the garlic, tomatoes, reserved tomato juice, sugar, basil, and seasonings. Over a medium heat, cook until sauce-like, stirring occasionally. Add the okra. Cover and cook gently for 15–20 minutes or until tender.

Po' Boy

The famous Po' Boy sandwich can contain any number of ingredients: the crusty hot French loaf can be stuffed with fried fish, oysters, roast beef and gravy, meatballs, or even French fries. A Po' Boy can be "dressed" with lettuce, tomato, and mayonnaise, but is just as appetizing and popular unadorned!

It is said the sandwich came into being in the 1920s when it cost a po' 5¢. Others say that the Cajun Martin brothers, who opened a restaurant in 1922 near the French Market, created the sandwich when they fed the men for free during a streetcar strike. Or it may have found its name in the French word *pourboire*, meaning a tip or gratuity. Like all New Orleans legends, the origins of the Po' Boy are probably a mixture of all of the above.

Oyster Po' Boy

---

1 loaf French bread or baguette, cut in half lengthwise
4 tbsp butter
24 small oysters, shucked and drained
cornmeal
oil for deep-frying
shredded lettuce
mayonnaise

Prehet oven to 375°F. Scoop out center from bottom half of loaf, brush both halves with melted butter and toast in the oven for about 10 minutes. Coat drained oysters in cornmeal and deep-fry in hot oil for 1–2 minutes. Drain on paper towels. Fill scooped-out half with oysters, top with shredded lettuce and mayonnaise. Close with other half of bread.

Cajun Cooking

Southwest of New Orleans is bayou country where the waters teem with seafood, waterfowl, and alligator. This is the homeland of the Cajuns, descendants of French colonists who were forcibly transported from Nova Scotia (which they called *l'Acadie*) in the 1750s when the British took over. The Acadians settled along the banks of the bayous and struggled to survive as fur trappers, wetland farmers, and fishermen. They didn't mix much with the city Creoles, despite sharing a common French heritage, as the Cajuns had their own customs and a language that was quite different from the Creole *patois*. This cultural isolation continued for over 200 years and, as a result, their style of cooking is unique.

One-pot dishes are traditional, and that one pot is likely to be a huge cast iron vessel, probably because Cajuns are very gregarious people who love all-night parties for their friends and extended families as much as they love food. The unpretentious homestyle cooking makes much use of lard, black pudding, and the garlicky *andouille* sausage – truly soul-satisfying. And spicing can be blisteringly hot: typically, three kinds of pepper (red cayenne, black, and white) are used to achieve the right balance of pepperiness in a dish, plus Tabasco sauce from nearby Avery Island. According to Paul Prudhomme, the world famous Cajun chef, hot spicing is essential in a humid climate because it makes you sweat so much that you cool off faster!

Crawfish Étouffée

Crawfish (called crayfish by the rest of the world) are cheap and abundant when in season. One popular way to prepare them is smothered with a blanket of chopped vegetables in a rich and spicy redbrown sauce. This recipe serves the *étouffée* over plain or buttered long-grain rice.

6 tbsp lard or vegetable oil	1 tbsp lemon juice
4 tbsp flour	1/2 tsp cayenne pepper
2 onions, chopped	1/2 tsp each black and white pepper
2 celery stalks, chopped	salt to taste
1/2 red pepper, chopped	2 lb peeled crawfish tails, with
1/2 green pepper, chopped	crawfish fat if available
2 garlic cloves, finely chopped	chopped spring onions or scallions
about 2 1/2 cups fish stock or water	parsley to finish
2 tbsp tomato paste	

Heat the lard in a large heavy pot, add the flour and stir over low heat until the *roux* is the pale brown color of hazelnut shells. Add the chopped vegetables and garlic. Cook until the vegetables are soft, stirring frequently. Slowly stir in the fish stock, then add the tomato paste, lemon juice, and seasonings. Bring to a boil and simmer for 20 minutes. Add the crawfish tails and fat, plus a little more stock or water if the sauce is very thick. Simmer for 5–10 minutes or until the tails are just tender. Stir in spring onions and parsley and serve over rice.

Red Beans and Rice

Monday was wash-day in old Creole and Cajun households. The lengthy chore of boiling and scrubbing left little time or energy for cooking, so a big pot of beans was put on the fire to simmer until the laundry was all dry and folded. Even today, many families in New Orleans sit down to a dinner of red beans and rice on Monday nights, just as their ancestors did.

---

1 lb dried red kidney beans, soaked overnight
2 tbsp bacon drippings or vegetable oil
2 onions, chopped
2 celery stalks, chopped
2 garlic cloves, chopped
1 large green pepper, chopped
4 tbsp each chopped parsley and spring onions or scallions
1 meaty ham bone or small bacon knuckle or ham hock, cut into 3 or 4 pieces

8 oz each baked ham and pickled pork or salt pork, cut into chunks
2 1/2 qts water
1 tbsp Worcestershire sauce
1/2 tsp each black pepper and cayenne pepper
1/2 tsp dried thyme
salt to taste
boiled rice to serve
spring onions and parsley to garnish

In a saucepan, cover the beans with fresh water and boil for 10 minutes. Drain. Heat the drippings or oil in a large heavy pot and sweat the chopped vegetables and garlic until soft. Add the beans and remaining ingredients (except salt). Bring to a boil, skimming the surface occasionally to remove froth, then half cover the saucepan and simmer for 3–3 1/2 hours or until the beans are tender and the liquid has reduced to a thick gravy. Stir from time to time

and add salt to taste. To serve, ladle the beans over hot rice and sprinkle with some chopped scallions and parsley.

Broiled Redfish Fillets with Spiced Butter

Redfish has firm flesh, so it can be cooked in all sorts of ways – broiled, baked, poached, or fried. It's the fish made famous by Cajun chef Paul Prudhomme, who was the first to coat it with a blisteringly hot spice mixture before pan-frying it. Here, spices are incorporated into a basting sauce for broiled fillets. If you can't get redfish, you can prepare sea bass, whiting, or rockfish fillets in the same way. Fillets should be $^{1}/_{2}$–$^{3}/_{4}$ inches thick.

6 tbsp butter	$^{1}/_{4}$ tsp white pepper
1 tbsp lemon juice	2 small to medium redfish,
$^{1}/_{2}$ tsp Tabasco or more to taste	filleted and skinned
$^{1}/_{2}$ tsp salt	lemon wedges to serve

Preheat the broiler. Melt the butter in a small saucepan. Remove from the heat and stir in the lemon juice, Tabasco, salt, and pepper. Keep warm. Arrange the redfish fillets on a rack in the broiler pan. Drizzle a little of the spiced butter over them. Place under the broiler, 3–4 inches from the heat, and broil for 6–7 minutes. There is no need to turn the fillets. They should be removed from the heat when the flesh is still slightly translucent in the center as they will continue to cook for another minute or so.

Transfer the fillets to serving plates. Quickly reheat the spiced butter, spoon it over the fish and serve, garnished with lemon wedges.

Gumbo

Gumbo, a thick soup made from whatever is to hand in the kitchen, is the very essence of the "melting pot" that is the city of New Orleans: it has absorbed influences from the French (who gave it the *roux*), the Spanish (who gave it peppers), the Africans (who gave it its name, the African word for okra), the West Indians (who added hot spices), and the Native Americans (who gave it the alternative thickener, *filé* powder, ground from dried sassafras leaves).

It is the *roux* base that gives gumbo its dark mystery and smoky taste. It is said that the Creoles favor a light golden brown *roux* made with butter while the Cajuns like a dark rich brown *roux* made with lard or duck fat. The art of a good *roux* is very slow cooking, constantly stirring to toast the flour. Then mix in the "Holy Trinity" of onions, green pepper, and celery, plus your favorite ingredients, cast your own special *gris-gris* spell, and enjoy.

Filé Gumbo

1/2 cup vegetable oil or lard	1 bay leaf
3–31/2 lb chicken, cut into 8 pieces	1/2 tsp each black pepper, white pepper and cayenne pepper
6 tbsp flour	salt
1 large onion, finely chopped	Tabasco to taste
1 celery stalk, finely chopped	about 5 cups chicken stock or water
1 green pepper, finely chopped	
1/2 bunch spring onions, finely chopped	1 dozen freshly shucked oysters, with their juice
1–2 garlic cloves, finely chopped	2 tbsp filé powder to taste (more can be added if desired)
2 tbsp chopped parsley	
4 oz smoked ham, diced	boiled rice to serve
8 oz smoked sausage, sliced	
1 tsp dried thyme	

Heat the oil in a large heavy pot and brown the chicken pieces. Remove chicken and set aside. Add the flour to the pot and stir over low heat until the *roux* is the pale brown color of hazelnut shells. Add the chopped vegetables, garlic, and parsley and cook until soft. Stir in the ham and sausage. Cook, stirring, for 3–4 minutes. Add the seasonings (except the *filé* powder) and gradually stir in the stock or water. Add the oyster juice and bring to a boil. Return the chicken to the pot and simmer for 1 hour. Stir frequently. Add the oysters and simmer for 5 minutes or until the edges start to curl. Remove from the heat and stir in the *filé* powder. Serve over boiled rice.

Barbecue Shrimp

Despite the name, these shrimp never come near a charcoal fire. They are, in fact, whole shrimp in their shells cooked in a very peppery butter sauce. This Italian-Creole dish was made famous by Pascal Manale's restaurant on Napoleon Avenue, though now you can find it everywhere. It's easy to make at home. If you can only get headless shrimp, use 3 lb.

---

1 1/2 sticks butter	1/2 tsp dried basil
1/2 cup olive oil	1/2 tsp oregano
1/2 cup dry white wine	3 bay leaves
3 tbsp fresh lemon juice	Tabasco
2 garlic cloves, finely chopped	salt and black pepper to taste
1 tsp dried thyme	6 lb raw shrimp or prawns in
1 tsp dried rosemary	shell, with heads
1/2 tsp cayenne pepper	French bread
(serves 4–6)	

Preheat oven to 425°F. Put all the ingredients, except the shrimp, in a saucepan and bring to a boil. Reduce the heat and simmer for 5 minutes. Remove from heat and leave to infuse for 30 minutes. Stir the shrimp into the sauce and pour into a baking dish. Bake for about 10 minutes or until the shrimp shells have turned pink. Serve hot, with French bread for mopping up the spicy butter sauce.

Fried Soft-Shell Crabs

Crabs are prepared in every conceivable way in New Orleans, from the simplest crab boil to elegant sauced preparations of the luscious meat. In the spring, the greatest delicacy of all arrives when the native blue crabs shed their shells.

4 large or 8 small soft-shell crabs	$^1/_4$ tsp cayenne pepper
buttermilk or milk	$^1/_4$ tsp black pepper
1 $^1/_2$ cups all-purpose flour	$^1/_4$ tsp white pepper
1 tsp salt	oil for deep frying

Soft-shell crabs should be cleaned just before cooking. With scissors, snip off $^1/_2$ inch of front of head to remove eyes. Pull out small greyish sac behind eye cavity and discard. Lift up pointed soft top shell on one side and pull off the spongy "dead man's fingers" that are underneath; replace shell. Repeat on other side. Pull off triangular-shaped piece from underside. Rinse crab well under cold running water and pat dry gently.

Cover crabs in buttermilk or milk and set aside to soak for 10–15 minutes. Mix flour with seasonings on a plate or sheet of paper. Heat oil to 375°F. Drain crabs, one at a time, then coat all over with seasoned flour, handling crabs carefully so you don't crush them.

Fry one or two at a time for 5–10 minutes or until they are deep golden brown, turning so they color evenly. Drain on paper towels. Keep hot, uncovered, in the oven until all are fried. Serve hot, with tartare sauce.

Crabmeat Imperial

In the early nineteenth century, the only place to eat in public was in elegant hotel dining rooms where rich, European-style food was served. Later, more modest eating places opened, offering good Creole cooking. This dish harks back to that early grand restaurant tradition, but with Creole refinements.

---

1 bunch of spring onions or scallions (white parts), finely chopped
3 tbsp celery, finely chopped
3 tbsp green pepper, finely chopped
2 tbsp butter
3 tbsp medium-dry sherry
1 cup whipping cream
1 egg yolk
salt and freshly ground pepper to taste
12 oz fresh lump crabmeat
fine breadcrumbs
freshly grated Parmesan cheese for the top
scallop shells (optional)

In a medium saucepan over medium heat, soften the spring onions, celery, and green pepper in the butter. Add the sherry and boil until almost completely evaporated. Stir in the cream and boil to reduce for 4–5 minutes. In a separate bowl, mix a little of the hot cream into the egg yolk, then stir this into the remaining cream mixture in the pan. Remove from heat and season. Reserve 4 tablespoons sauce and fold the crabmeat into the remainder. Divide among 4 buttered scallop shells or other small dishes. Top with the reserved sauce and sprinkle crumbs and cheese on top. Finish under the broiler to brown the top lightly.

King Cake

On January 6, when the Christmas festivities wind down in New Orleans, the carnival season begins. The dizzying round of parties and events will eventually culminate in the famous explosion of color and music that is *Mardi Gras.*

At the start of Carnival, which falls on Twelfth Night, the first King Cake is served, at a party or masked ball (or even just at the office). This brioche-type ring can contain walnuts and candied fruit, or a praline or whiskey filling, and it has a garish icing tinted with the traditional carnival colors of purple, green, and gold. Hidden in the cake's rich interior is a tiny toy doll or a red bean wrapped in silver or gold leaf. The lucky one who finds the doll or bean becomes the king or queen of the evening and is obliged to host the next event (or buy the next cake). It is little wonder that some exhausted "winners" choose to swallow the token!

Some say the cake's origins date from a pre-Christian fertility rite, with the token symbolizing new life, and similar cakes can be found throughout Europe. But in New Orleans the King Cake has been firmly associated with boisterous revelry for at least 120 years.

King Cake is seldom baked at home today, but throughout the Carnival season it is ubiquitous in the city's bakeries.

Oysters Rockefeller

When Antoine's first opened, it was a boarding house with a public dining room that served good food without frills. Due to its popularity, the dining room became a restaurant. It is still open and is now New Orleans' oldest French Creole restaurant. Among the many classic dishes that were created there over the years is this oyster dish, named as such because it is so rich.

1 celery stalk, chopped
1 small bunch spring onions or scallions, chopped
4 tbsp chopped parsley
1 stick butter
1 lb fresh spinach leaves, chopped
1 bunch watercress leaves
3 tbsp Herbsaint or Pernod
1 tbsp Worcestershire sauce
cayenne pepper, salt, and black pepper to taste
2 dozen fresh raw oysters, on the half shell, juice reserved
rock salt (optional)

Preheat oven to 400°F. In a skillet, soften the celery, spring onions, and parsley in the butter. Add the spinach and watercress and cook until wilted. Add the reserved oyster juice. Boil until excess liquid has evaporated, stirring frequently. Purée in a food processor or blender. Add the Herbsaint or Pernod, Worcestershire sauce, and seasonings. Arrange the oysters in one layer in a shallow pan (ideally on a bed of rock salt to keep them steady). Spoon the spinach sauce over the oysters. Bake for about 10 minutes or until the edges of the oysters are curling and the sauce is bubbling. Serve hot.

Pompano en Papillote

In 1901, the French balloonist Alberto Santos-Dumont was visiting New Orleans. In his honor, the chef at Antoine's baked a delectable pompano fillet in a paper parcel that puffed up to resemble a turn-of-the-century flying balloon.

---

2 tbsp butter
2–3 spring onions or scallions, chopped
1 tbsp flour
½ cup fish stock
4 tbsp dry white wine
4 tbsp whipping cream
lemon juice
salt and pepper to taste
1 egg yolk
4 oz mushrooms, sliced and sautéed in butter
6 oz each fresh lump crabmeat and peeled
cooked small shrimp or prawns
4 skinned pompano fillets (or trout, red snapper, or small sea bass)

Melt the butter in a saucepan and soften the spring onions. Add the flour and cook, stirring, for 1 minute. Gradually stir in the fish stock, wine, and cream. Simmer for 5 minutes, stirring frequently. Season to taste. In a separate bowl, mix a little of the hot sauce into the egg yolk, then stir yolk into the remaining sauce. Remove from heat and fold in the mushrooms, crabmeat, and shrimp. Cut out 4 large heart shapes (12 inches across) from parchment paper. Butter them and crease in half. Put a spoonful of sauce on half of each heart, put a fish fillet on top and cover with the remaining sauce. Fold over the paper, then seal the edges by folding them

over twice. Set on a baking sheet and bake at 400°F for 15–20 minutes. Serve in the paper.

Bananas Foster

New Orleanians love dramatic flambéed desserts, particularly when dining out on special occasions, and this is one of the most famous of those sweets. It was created at Brennan's restaurant, and was named for Dick Foster, vice-chairman of the committee that was given the task of cleaning up crime in the French Quarter in the 1950s.

---

4 tbsp unsalted butter
$\frac{1}{2}$ cup light brown sugar, packed
$\frac{1}{2}$ tsp ground cinnamon
4 large bananas, halved lengthwise and then across
6 tbsp banana liqueur
6 tbsp rum
4 large scoops vanilla ice cream

Melt the butter in a large flambé pan or skillet. Add the sugar and cinnamon and stir until smooth. Add the bananas and the banana liqueur and sauté until they begin to soften. Pour in the rum and heat it briefly, then ignite with a long-handled match. Continue to cook, basting the bananas with the sauce with a long-handled spoon, until the flames die out. Using a large spoon, lift the pieces of banana on to serving plates and top each portion with a large scoop of ice cream. Spoon the hot sauce over and serve immediately.

Bread Pudding with Bourbon Sauce

What was devised as a way for frugal Creole cooks to use up stale French bread has become a sublime dessert. It must be that rich alcoholic sauce!

12 inch day-old French bread, torn in small pieces	3 eggs, beaten (jumbo)
about 1 1/2 cups milk	1/2 cup chopped toasted pecans
about 1 1/2 cups whipping cream	4 tbsp unsalted butter
3/4 cup granulated sugar	3/4 cup light brown sugar, packed
1 tsp grated orange zest	2/3 cup light cream
1 tsp vanilla extract	4 tbsp bourbon whiskey, or more to taste

(serves 6–8)

Preheat oven to 350°F. Put the bread in a bowl. Warm the milk and cream in a saucepan and stir in the granulated sugar until dissolved. Add the orange zest, vanilla extract, and eggs. Pour over the bread and soak for 15–20 minutes. Stir in the pecans. Add more milk if bread looks a little dry. Turn into a buttered shallow baking dish. Set the dish in a large pan of hot water and bake for 40–45 minutes or until firm and light golden brown. Cool until warm. Heat the butter in a small saucepan with the brown sugar until smooth. Boil for 1 minute. Remove the syrup from heat and stir in the cream and bourbon. Cut the pudding into squares and spoon over the bourbon sauce.

Pecan Pralines

The pralines of New Orleans are rich and buttery, with a soft fudge-like texture quite unlike the hard praline of France. They are irresistible, particularly when freshly made and still warm.

---

1 1/2 cups granulated sugar
1 1/2 cups brown sugar, packed
1/2 cup milk
1/2 cup whipping cream
1/4 tsp salt
1/4 tsp cream of tartar
4 tbsp unsalted butter
1 1/2 tsp vanilla extract
2 cups pecan halves
(makes approx. 30)

Put the sugars, milk, cream, salt and cream of tartar in a heavy, deep saucepan and heat, stirring to dissolve the sugars. Once dissolved, bring to a boil. Stop stirring and boil to the soft ball stage (238°F). Remove from heat and let the bubbles subside, then stir in the butter, vanilla extract, and pecans. Beat with a wooden spoon for a few minutes until the mixture starts to cool and look creamy. Quickly drop tablespoonfuls on to buttered foil or wax paper, leaving room for spreading. Pralines will set as they cool. They are best when freshly made.

Absinthe Ice Cream

In the mid-1800s an anise-flavored liquor called *absinthe* became very popular in the bars and cafés of New Orleans. However, many of its devotees went mad or died. As a result, *absinthe* was banned: it used wormwood in its distillation, which was declared an addictive narcotic. Today's *absinthe* substitutes, such as locally produced Herbsaint and French Pernod, are made without wormwood.

---

4 egg yolks	2 cups heavy cream
³/₄ cup sugar	4 tbsp Herbsaint or Pernod
2 cups milk	

Beat the egg yolks with the sugar until pale and thickened. Heat the milk in the top pan of a double boiler until bubbles appear around the edge. Stir the hot milk into the egg yolk mixture, then pour back into the pan. Set over the bottom pan containing just simmering water and cook, stirring, until the custard thickens to a creamy consistency that will coat the spoon. Remove from heat and stir in the cream and liqueur. Cool to room temperature, then pour into an ice cream machine and freeze until firm.

Drinks

Sazerac
At the Sazerac Bar in the Fairmont Hotel, the preparation of the cocktail is impressive: the barman puts the anise liquor in a glass, throws it in the air, where it twists and turns, coating the glass with the liquor, and then catches it.

1 tsp superfine sugar	1 oz bourbon
1 tsp water	1 tsp Herbsaint or Pernod
2 drops Peychaud	a twist of lemon peel
2 drops Angostura bitters	

Put the sugar and water in a cocktail shaker and stir to dissolve the sugar. Add the bitters and bourbon. Pour the Herbsaint into a chilled old-fashioned glass and tilt and turn it to coat the inside all over. Pour out excess. Stir the ingredients in the cocktail shaker and strain into the glass. Add a lemon twist and serve.

Café Brûlot

Very strong, rich chicory coffee is preferred in New Orleans (coffee without chicory is called "Northern coffee"). A fitting finalé to a fine meal is this classic coffee concoction, traditionally prepared in a heavy copper *brûlot* bowl.

fine strips of zest from	6 tbsp brandy
1 orange and 1/2 lemon	2 tbsp orange liqueur
1 cinnamon stick	2 cups hot strong black
4 whole cloves	chicory coffee
2 1/2 tbsp sugar	

Put the zest into a *brûlot* bowl or chafing dish and add the spices and sugar. Mash together to crush and release the oils. Add the brandy and liqueur and heat to boiling point. Ignite with a long handled match. Stir with a long-handled spoon to dissolve the sugar. When the flames begin to subside, gradually stir in the hot coffee. Ladle into *brûlot* cups or *demitasses* and serve.

Index